A DICTIONARY OF INTERNATIONAL UNITS

Metric-Matters: Names and Symbols

Philip Bladon

R389·15

iUniverse, Inc.
New York Lincoln Shanghai

A Dictionary Of International Units
Metric-Matters: Names and Symbols

iUniverse books may be ordered through booksellers or by contacting:

iUniverse
2021 Pine Lake Road, Suite 100
Lincoln, NE 68512
www.iuniverse.com
1-800-Authors (1-800-288-4677)

ISBN-13: 978-0-595-37115-0 (pbk)
ISBN-13: 978-0-595-81515-9 (ebk)
ISBN-10: 0-595-37115-9 (pbk)
ISBN-10: 0-595-81515-4 (ebk)

Printed in the United States of America

A DICTIONARY OF
INTERNATIONAL UNITS

To: "Kg" and "Km"

"You're in<u>k</u>orrect"

ACKNOWLEDGEMENT

Grateful thanks to Mrs Valerie Kotkin-Smith, <u>charlesk36@</u> <u>hotmail.com</u>, for her assistance with typing.

CONTENTS

This dictionary caters for browsers and for people searching for particular SI unit names and symbols.

INTRODUCTION

Welcome to Metric-Matters, archive your 'old' units and brighten up the future with SI. For extremely high illumination **yottalux** is the unit to use.

This dictionary provides information for everyone; trivia and Scrabble® buffs can enrich their vocabulary; symbologists and symbolists can ponder over the character sizes. Do you know the meaning of **Zs'**, **'zs'**, **ZS'** and **'zS'**?

Metric-Matters introduces you to 'Le Système International d'Unités' (designated SI in all languages). **This is the International Standard.**

Students, especially those studying science, will find this dictionary a valuable reference book throughout their careers.

My aim in compiling this dictionary is not only to provide a valuable resource for reference, for scientists and students alike, but also to present a work that offers guidance on how to write units, names, symbols, and numerical values correctly.

Thank you.

Philip Bladon

PART ONE

Symbols → Names

A	ampere	**am**	attometre
a	*the prefix 'atto'*	**amol**	attomole
aA	attoampere	**aN**	attonewton
aBq	attobecquerel	**aΩ**	attoohm
aC	attocoulomb	**aPa**	attopascal
acd	attocandela	**arad**	attoradian
aF	attofarad	**aS**	attosiemens
aGy	attogray	**as**	attosecond
ag	attogram	**asr**	attosteradian
aH	attohenry	**aSv**	attosievert
aHz	attohertz	**aT**	attotesla
aJ	attojoule	**aV**	attovolt
aK	attokelvin	**aW**	attowatt
alm	attolumen	**aWb**	attoweber
alx	attolux		

> *Symbols must remain unaltered in the plural. DO NOT ADD 's', "ms" refers to millisecond **not metres**.*

> *Unit names must not begin with a capital letter.*

> *Prefixes must only be used when combined with a unit.*

Bq	becquerel	**clx**	centilux
		cm	centimetre
C	coulomb	**cmol**	centimole
°C	degree Celsius	**cN**	centinewton
cd	candela	**cΩ**	centiohm
c	*the prefix 'centi'*	**cPa**	centipascal
cA	centiampere	**crad**	centiradian
cBq	centibecquerel	**cS**	centisiemens
cC	centicoulomb	**cs**	centisecond
ccd	centicandela	**csr**	centisteradian
cF	centifarad	**cSv**	centisievert
cGy	centigray	**cT**	centitesla
cg	centigram	**cV**	centivolt
cH	centihenry	**cW**	centiwatt
cHz	centihertz	**cWb**	centiweber
cJ	centijoule		
cK	centikelvin	*d*	*the prefix 'deci'*
clm	centilumen	**dA**	deciampere

> *Symbols must remain unaltered in the plural. DO NOT ADD 's', "ms" refers to millisecond **not metres**.*

> *Unit names must not begin with a capital letter.*

> *Prefixes must only be used when combined with a unit.*

da	the prefix *'deca'* see later entries	**drad**	deciradian
dBq	decibecquerel	**dS**	decisiemens
dC	decicoulomb	**ds**	decisecond
dcd	decicandela	**dsr**	decisteradian
dF	decifarad	**dSv**	decisievert
dGy	decigray	**dT**	decitesla
dg	decigram	**dV**	decivolt
dH	decihenry	**dW**	deciwatt
dHz	decihertz	**dWb**	deciweber
dJ	decijoule	*da*	the prefix *'deca'*
dK	decikelvin	**daA**	decaampere
dlm	decilumen	**daBq**	decabecquerel
dlx	decilux	**daC**	decacoulomb
dm	decimetre	**dacd**	decacandela
dmol	decimole	**daF**	decafarad
dN	decinewton	**daGy**	decagray
dΩ	deciohm	**dag**	decagram
dPa	decipascal	**daH**	decahenry

> *Symbols must remain unaltered in the plural. DO NOT ADD 's', "ms" refers to millisecond **not metres**.*

> *Unit names must not begin with a capital letter.*

> *Prefixes must only be used when combined with a unit.*

daHz	decahertz		**daWb**	decaweber
daJ	decajoule			
daK	decakelvin		*E*	*the prefix 'exa'*
dalm	decalumen		**EA**	exaampere
dalx	decalux		**EBq**	exabecquerel
dam	decametre		**EC**	exacoulomb
damol	decamole		**Ecd**	exacandela
daN	decanewton		**EF**	exafarad
daΩ	decaohm		**EGy**	exagray
daPa	decapascal		**Eg**	exagram
darad	decaradian		**EH**	exahenry
daS	decasiemens		**EHz**	exahertz
das	decasecond		**EJ**	exajoule
dasr	decasteradian		**EK**	exakelvin
daSv	decasievert		**Elm**	exalumen
daT	decatesla		**Elx**	exalux
daV	decavolt		**Em**	exametre
daW	decawatt		**Emol**	examole

> *Symbols must remain unaltered in the plural. DO NOT ADD 's', "ms" refers to millisecond **not metres**.*

> *Unit names must not begin with a capital letter.*

> *Prefixes must only be used when combined with a unit.*

EN	exanewton		**fcd**	femtocandela
EΩ	exaohm		**fF**	femtofarad
EPa	exapascal		**fGy**	femtogray
Erad	exaradian		**fg**	femtogram
ES	exasiemens		**fH**	femtohenry
Es	exasecond		**fHz**	femtohertz
Esr	exasteradian		**fJ**	femtojoule
ESv	exasievert		**fK**	femtokelvin
ET	exatesla		**flm**	femtolumen
EV	exavolt		**flx**	femtolux
EW	exawatt		**fm**	femtometre
EWb	exaweber		**fmol**	femtomole
			fN	femtonewton
F	farad		**fΩ**	femtoohm
f	*the prefix 'femto'*		**fPa**	femtopascal
fA	femtoampere		**frad**	femtoradian
fBq	femtobecquerel		**fS**	femtosiemens
fC	femtocoulomb		**fs**	femtosecond

> *Symbols must remain unaltered in the plural. DO NOT ADD 's', "ms" refers to millisecond **not metres.***

> *Unit names must not begin with a capital letter.*

> *Prefixes must only be used when combined with a unit.*

fsr	femtosteradian		**GHz**	gigahertz
fSv	femtosievert		**GJ**	gigajoule
fT	femtotesla		**GK**	gigakelvin
fV	femtovolt		**Glm**	gigalumen
fW	femtowatt		**Glx**	gigalux
fWb	femtoweber		**Gm**	gigametre
			Gmol	gigamole
g	gram		**GN**	giganewton
Gy	gray		**GΩ**	gigaohm
G	*the prefix 'giga'*		**GPa**	gigapascal
GA	gigaampere		**Grad**	gigaradian
GBq	gigabecquerel		**GS**	gigasiemens
GC	gigacoulomb		**Gs**	gigasecond
Gcd	gigacandela		**Gsr**	gigasteradian
GF	gigafarad		**GSv**	gigasievert
GGy	gigagray		**GT**	gigatesla
Gg	gigagram		**GV**	gigavolt
GH	gigahenry		**GW**	gigawatt

> *Symbols must remain unaltered in the plural. DO NOT ADD 's', "ms" refers to millisecond **not metres**.*

> *Unit names must not begin with a capital letter.*

> *Prefixes must only be used when combined with a unit.*

GWb	gigaweber		**hm**	hectometre
			hmol	hectomole
H	henry		**hN**	hectonewton
Hz	hertz		**hΩ**	hectoohm
h	*the prefix 'hecto'*		**hPa**	hectopascal
hA	hectoampere		**hrad**	hectoradian
hBq	hectobecquerel		**hS**	hectosiemens
hC	hectocoulomb		**hs**	hectosecond
hcd	hectocandela		**hsr**	hectosteradian
hF	hectofarad		**hSv**	hectosievert
hGy	hectogray		**hT**	hectotesla
hg	hectogram		**hV**	hectovolt
hH	hectohenry		**hW**	hectowatt
hHz	hectohertz		**hWb**	hectoweber
hJ	hectojoule			
hK	hectokelvin		**J**	joule
hlm	hectolumen			
hlx	hectolux			

> *Symbols must remain unaltered in the plural. DO NOT ADD 's', "ms" refers to millisecond **not metres.***

> *Unit names must not begin with a capital letter.*

> *Prefixes must only be used when combined with a unit.*

K	kelvin; note, it is *incorrect* to write '°K', compare with degree Celsius '°C'	**kmol**	kilomole
		kN	kilonewton
		kΩ	kiloohm
k	*the prefix 'kilo'*	**kPa**	kilopascal
kA	kiloampere	**krad**	kiloradian
kBq	kilobecquerel	**kS**	kilosiemens
kC	kilocoulomb	**ks**	kilosecond
kcd	kilocandela	**ksr**	kilosteradian
kF	kilofarad	**kSv**	kilosievert
kGy	kilogray	**kT**	kilotesla
kg	kilogram	**kV**	kilovolt
kH	kilohenry	**kW**	kilowatt
kHz	kilohertz	**kWb**	kiloweber
kJ	kilojoule		
kK	kilokelvin	**lm**	lumen
klm	kilolumen	**lx**	lux
klx	kilolux		
km	kilometre	**m**	metre

> *Symbols must remain unaltered in the plural. DO NOT ADD 's', "ms" refers to millisecond **not metres.***

> *Unit names must not begin with a capital letter.*

> *Prefixes must only be used when combined with a unit.*

m	*the prefix 'milli' see later entries*	**Mm**	megametre
μ	*the prefix 'micro' see later entries*	**Mmol**	megamole
		MN	meganewton
mol	mole	**MΩ**	megaohm
M	*the prefix 'mega'*	**MPa**	megapascal
MA	megaampere	**Mrad**	megaradian
MBq	megabecquerel	**MS**	megasiemens
MC	megacoulomb	**Ms**	megasecond
Mcd	megacandela	**Msr**	megasteradian
MF	megafarad	**MSv**	megasievert
MGy	megagray	**MT**	megatesla
Mg	megagram	**MV**	megavolt
MH	megahenry	**MW**	megawatt
MHz	megahertz	**MWb**	megaweber
MJ	megajoule		
MK	megakelvin		
Mlm	megalumen		
Mlx	megalux		

> *Symbols must remain unaltered in the plural. DO NOT ADD 's', "ms" refers to millisecond **not metres.***

> *Unit names must not begin with a capital letter.*

> *Prefixes must only be used when combined with a unit.*

m	the prefix 'milli'	**mlx**	millilux

NOTE: if the symbol **'m'** is used by itself or used after one or more symbols **'m'** refers to 'metre', examples: **'m'** (metre), **'cm'** (centimetre).

		mm	millimetre
		mmol	millimole
		mN	millinewton
		mΩ	milliohm
		mPa	millipascal
mA	milliampere	**mrad**	milliradian
mBq	millibecquerel	**mS**	millisiemens
mC	millicoulomb	**ms**	millisecond
mcd	millicandela	**msr**	millisteradian
mF	millifarad	**mSv**	millisievert
mGy	milligray	**mT**	millitesla
mg	milligram	**mV**	millivolt
mH	millihenry	**mW**	milliwatt
mHz	millihertz	**mWb**	milliweber
mJ	millijoule	*µ*	the prefix 'micro'
mK	millikelvin	**µA**	microampere
mlm	millilumen	**µBq**	microbecquerel

> *Symbols must remain unaltered in the plural. DO NOT ADD 's', "ms" refers to millisecond **not metres**.*

> *Unit names must not begin with a capital letter.*

> *Prefixes must only be used when combined with a unit.*

μC	microcoulomb		**μs**	microsecond
μcd	microcandela		**μsr**	microsteradian
μF	microfarad		**μSv**	microsievert
μGy	microgray		**μT**	microtesla
μg	microgram		**μV**	microvolt
μH	microhenry		**μW**	microwatt
μHz	microhertz		**μWb**	microweber
μJ	microjoule			
μK	microkelvin		**N**	newton
μlm	microlumen		*n*	*the prefix 'nano'*
μlx	microlux		**nA**	nanoampere
μm	micrometre		**nBq**	nanobecquerel
μmol	micromole		**nC**	nanocoulomb
μN	micronewton		**ncd**	nanocandela
μΩ	microohm		**nF**	nanofarad
μPa	micropascal		**nGy**	nanogray
μrad	microradian		**ng**	nanogram
μS	microsiemens		**nH**	nanohenry

> *Symbols must remain unaltered in the plural. DO NOT ADD 's', "ms" refers to millisecond **not metres**.*

> *Unit names must not begin with a capital letter.*

> *Prefixes must only be used when combined with a unit.*

nHz	nanohertz	**nWb**	nanoweber
nJ	nanojoule		
nK	nanokelvin	Ω	ohm
nlm	nanolumen		
nlx	nanolux	**Pa**	pascal
nm	nanometre	*P*	*the prefix 'peta'*
nmol	nanomole	**PA**	petaampere
nN	nanonewton	**PBq**	petabecquerel
nΩ	nanoohm	**PC**	petacoulomb
nPa	nanopascal	**Pcd**	petacandela
nrad	nanoradian	**PF**	petafarad
nS	nanosiemens	**PGy**	petagray
ns	nanosecond	**Pg**	petagram
nsr	nanosteradian	**PH**	petahenry
nSv	nanosievert	**PHz**	petahertz
nT	nanotesla	**PJ**	petajoule
nV	nanovolt	**PK**	petakelvin
nW	nanowatt	**Plm**	petalumen

> *Symbols must remain unaltered in the plural. DO NOT ADD 's', "ms" refers to millisecond **not metres**.*

> *Unit names must not begin with a capital letter.*

> *Prefixes must only be used when combined with a unit.*

Plx	petalux	**pC**	picocoulomb
Pm	petametre	**pcd**	picocandela
Pmol	petamole	**pF**	picofarad
PN	petanewton	**pGy**	picogray
PΩ	petaohm	**pg**	picogram
PPa	petapascal	**pH**	picohenry
Prad	petaradian	**pHz**	picohertz
PS	petasiemens	**pJ**	picojoule
Ps	petasecond	**pK**	picokelvin
Psr	petasteradian	**plm**	picolumen
PSv	petasievert	**plx**	picolux
PT	petatesla	**pm**	picometre
PV	petavolt	**pmol**	picomole
PW	petawatt	**pN**	piconewton
PWb	petaweber	**pΩ**	picoohm
p	*the prefix 'pico'*	**pPa**	picopascal
pA	picoampere	**prad**	picoradian
pBq	picobecquerel	**pS**	picosiemens

> *Symbols must remain unaltered in the plural. DO NOT ADD 's', "ms" refers to millisecond **not metres.***

> *Unit names must not begin with a capital letter.*

> *Prefixes must only be used when combined with a unit.*

ps	picosecond	*T*	*the prefix 'tera'*
psr	picosteradian		**NOTE:** if the symbol 'T' is
pSv	picosievert		used by itself or used after
pT	picotesla		another symbol, the 'T'
pV	picovolt		refers to 'tesla', examples: 'T'
pW	picowatt		(tesla), 'nT' (nanotesla).
pWb	picoweber	**TA**	teraampere
		TBq	terabecquerel
rad	radian	**TC**	teracoulomb
		Tcd	teracandela
S	siemens	**TF**	terafarad
s	second	**TGy**	teragray
sr	steradian	**Tg**	teragram
Sv	sievert	**TH**	terahenry
		THz	terahertz
T	tesla	**TJ**	terajoule
		TK	terakelvin
		Tlm	teralumen

> *Symbols must remain unaltered in the plural. DO NOT ADD 's', "ms" refers to millisecond **not metres**.*

> *Unit names must not begin with a capital letter.*

> *Prefixes must only be used when combined with a unit.*

Tlx	teralux	**W**	watt
Tm	terametre	**Wb**	weber
Tmol	teramole		
TN	teranewton	*Y*	*the prefix 'yotta'*
TΩ	teraohm	**Y**	yottaampere
TPa	terapascal	**YBq**	yottabecquerel
Trad	teraradian	**YC**	yottacoulomb
TS	terasiemens	**Ycd**	yottacandela
Ts	terasecond	**YF**	yottafarad
Tsr	terasteradian	**YGy**	yottagray
TSv	terasievert	**Yg**	yottagram
TT	teratesla	**YH**	yottahenry
TV	teravolt	**YHz**	yottahertz
TW	terawatt	**YJ**	yottajoule
TWb	teraweber	**YK**	yottakelvin
		Ylm	yottalumen
V	volt	**Ylx**	yottalux
		Ym	yottametre

> *Symbols must remain unaltered in the plural. DO NOT ADD 's', "ms" refers to millisecond **not metres.***

> *Unit names must not begin with a capital letter.*

> *Prefixes must only be used when combined with a unit.*

Ymol	yottamole		**yF**	yoctofarad
YN	yottanewton		**yGy**	yoctogray
YΩ	yottaohm		**yg**	yoctogram
YPa	yottapascal		**yH**	yoctohenry
Yrad	yottaradian		**yHz**	yoctohertz
YS	yottasiemens		**yJ**	yoctojoule
Ys	yottasecond		**yK**	yoctokelvin
Ysr	yottasteradian		**ylm**	yoctolumen
YSv	yottasievert		**ylx**	yoctolux
YT	yottatesla		**ym**	yoctometre
YV	yottavolt		**ymol**	yoctomole
YW	yottawatt		**yN**	yoctonewton
YWb	yottaweber		**yΩ**	yoctoohm
y	*the prefix 'yocto'*		**yPa**	yoctopascal
yA	yoctoampere		**yrad**	yoctoradian
yBq	yoctobecquerel		**yS**	yoctosiemens
yC	yoctocoulomb		**ys**	yoctosecond
ycd	yoctocandela		**ysr**	yoctosteradian

> *Symbols must remain unaltered in the plural. DO NOT ADD 's', "ms" refers to millisecond **not metres.***

> *Unit names must not begin with a capital letter.*

> *Prefixes must only be used when combined with a unit.*

ySv	yoctosievert		**Zlm**	zettalumen
yT	yoctotesla		**Zlx**	zettalux
yV	yoctovolt		**Zm**	zettametre
yW	yoctowatt		**Zmol**	zettamole
yWb	yoctoweber		**ZN**	zettanewton
			ZΩ	zettaohm
Z	*the prefix 'zetta'*		**ZPa**	zettapascal
ZA	zettaampere		**Zrad**	zettaradian
ZBq	zettabecquerel		**ZS**	zettasiemens
ZC	zettacoulomb		**Zs**	zettasecond
Zcd	zettacandela		**Zsr**	zettasteradian
ZF	zettafarad		**ZSv**	zettasievert
ZGy	zettagray		**ZT**	zettatesla
Zg	zettagram		**ZV**	zettavolt
ZH	zettahenry		**ZW**	zettawatt
ZHz	zettahertz		**ZWb**	zettaweber
ZJ	zettajoule		*z*	*the prefix 'zepto'*
ZK	zettakelvin		**zA**	zeptoampere

> *Symbols must remain unaltered in the plural. DO NOT ADD 's', "ms" refers to millisecond **not metres**.*

> *Unit names must not begin with a capital letter.*

> *Prefixes must only be used when combined with a unit.*

zBq	zeptobecquerel		**zS**	zeptosiemens
zC	zeptocoulomb		**zs**	zeptosecond
zcd	zeptocandela		**zsr**	zeptosteradian
zF	zeptofarad		**zSv**	zeptosievert
zGy	zeptogray		**zT**	zeptotesla
zg	zeptogram		**zV**	zeptovolt
zH	zeptohenry		**zW**	zeptowatt
zHz	zeptohertz		**zWb**	zeptoweber
zJ	zeptojoule			
zK	zeptokelvin			
zlm	zeptolumen			
zlx	zeptolux			
zm	zeptometre			
zmol	zeptomole			
zN	zeptonewton			
zΩ	zeptoohm			
zPa	zeptopascal			
zrad	zeptoradian			

Names → Symbols

Prefixes must only be used when combined with a unit.

Symbols must remain unaltered in the plural. DO NOT ADD 's', "ms" refers to millisecond **not metres.**

ampere	A	**attonewton**	aN
atto +	*'a' ; 'atto' is a prefix*	**attoohm**	aΩ
attoampere	aA	**attopascal**	aPa
attobecquerel	aBq	**attoradian**	arad
attocandela	acd	**attosecond**	as
attocoulomb	aC	**attosiemens**	aS
attofarad	aF	**attosievert**	aSv
attogram	ag	**attosteradian**	asr
attogray	aGy	**attotesla**	aT
attohenry	aH	**attovolt**	aV
attohertz	aHz	**attowatt**	aW
attojoule	aJ	**attoweber**	aWb
attokelvin	aK		
attolumen	alm	**becquerel**	Bq
attolux	alx	**candela**	cd
attometre	am	*Celsius*	SEE LATER ENTRY
attomole	amol		degree Celsius

Unit names must not begin with a capital letter.

Prefixes must only be used when
combined with a unit.

Symbols must remain unaltered in the plural. DO
NOT ADD 's', "ms" refers to millisecond **not metres.**

centi +	*'c' ; 'centi' is a*	**centiohm**	cΩ
	prefix	**centipascal**	cPa
centiampere	cA	**centiradian**	crad
centibecquerel	cBq	**centisecond**	cs
centicandela	ccd	**centisiemens**	cS
centicoulomb	cC	**centisievert**	cSv
centifarad	cF	**centisteradian**	csr
centigram	cg	**centitesla**	cT
centigray	cGy	**centivolt**	cV
centihenry	cH	**centiwatt**	cW
centihertz	cHz	**centiweber**	cWb
centijoule	cJ	**coulomb**	C
centikelvin	cK		
centilumen	clm	*deca +*	*'da' ; 'deca' is a*
centilux	clx		*prefix*
centimetre	cm	**decaampere**	daA
centimole	cmol	**decabecquerel**	daBq
centinewton	cN	**decacandela**	dacd

Unit names must not begin with a capital letter.

Prefixes must only be used when
combined with a unit.

Symbols must remain unaltered in the plural. DO
NOT ADD 's', "ms" refers to millisecond **not metres.**

decacoulomb	daC	**decasievert**	daSv
decafarad	daF	**decasteradian**	dasr
decagram	dag	**decatesla**	daT
decagray	daGy	**decavolt**	daV
decahenry	daH	**decawatt**	daW
decahertz	daHz	**decaweber**	daWb
decajoule	daJ	*deci +*	'd' ; 'deci' is a prefix
decakelvin	daK	**deciampere**	dA
decalumen	dalm	**decibecquerel**	dBq
decalux	dalx	**decicandela**	dcd
decametre	dam	**decicoulomb**	dC
decamole	damol	**decifarad**	dF
decanewton	daN	**decigram**	dg
decaohm	daΩ	**decigray**	dGy
decapascal	daPa	**decihenry**	dH
decaradian	darad	**decihertz**	dHz
decasecond	das	**decijoule**	dJ
decasiemens	daS	**decikelvin**	dK

> Unit names must not begin with a capital letter.

> Prefixes must only be used when combined with a unit.

> Symbols must remain unaltered in the plural. DO NOT ADD 's', "ms" refers to millisecond **not metres.**

decilumen	dlm	**degree Celsius**	°C; "degree
decilux	dlx	Celsius" is a special name for the unit	
decimetre	dm	"kelvin".	
decimole	dmol		
decinewton	dN	_exa +_	_'E' ; 'exa' is a prefix_
deciohm	dΩ	**exaampere**	EA
decipascal	dPa	**exabecquerel**	EBq
deciradian	drad	**exacandela**	Ecd
decisecond	ds	**exacoulomb**	EC
decisiemens	dS	**exafarad**	EF
decisievert	dSv	**exagram**	Eg
decisteradian	dsr	**exagray**	EGy
decitesla	dT	**exahenry**	EH
decivolt	dV	**exahertz**	EHz
deciwatt	dW	**exajoule**	EJ
deciweber	dWb	**exakelvin**	EK
		exalumen	Elm

Unit names must not begin with a capital letter.	

Prefixes must only be used when combined with a unit.	

*Symbols must remain unaltered in the plural. DO NOT ADD 's', "ms" refers to millisecond **not metres**.*	

exalux	Elx	*femto +*	*'f' ; 'femto' is a*
exametre	Em		*prefix*
examole	Emol	**femtoampere**	fA
exanewton	EN	**femtobecquerel**	fBq
exaohm	EΩ	**femtocandela**	fcd
exapascal	EPa	**femtocoulomb**	fC
exaradian	Erad	**femtofarad**	fF
exasecond	Es	**femtogram**	fg
exasiemens	ES	**femtogray**	fGy
exasievert	ESv	**femtohenry**	fH
exasteradian	Esr	**femtohertz**	fHz
exatesla	ET	**femtojoule**	fJ
exavolt	EV	**femtokelvin**	fK
exawatt	EW	**femtolumen**	flm
exaweber	EWb	**femtolux**	flx
		femtometre	fm
farad	F	**femtomole**	fmol
		femtonewton	fN

> *Unit names must not begin with a capital letter.*

> *Prefixes must only be used when combined with a unit.*

> *Symbols must remain unaltered in the plural. DO NOT ADD 's', "ms" refers to millisecond **not metres**.*

femtoohm	fΩ		**gigafarad**	GF
femtopascal	fPa		**gigagram**	Gg
femtoradian	frad		**gigagray**	GGY
femtosecond	fs		**gigahenry**	GH
femtosiemens	fS		**gigahertz**	GHz
femtosievert	fSv		**gigajoule**	GJ
femtosteradian	fsr		**gigakelvin**	GK
femtotesla	fT		**gigalumen**	Glm
femtovolt	fV		**gigalux**	Glx
femtowatt	fW		**gigametre**	Gm
femtoweber	fWb		**gigamole**	Gmol
			giganewton	GN
giga +	*'G' ; 'giga' is a prefix*		**gigaohm**	GΩ
			gigapascal	GPa
gigaampere	GA		**gigaradian**	Grad
gigabecquerel	GBq		**gigasecond**	Gs
gigacandela	Gcd		**gigasiemens**	GS
gigacoulomb	GC		**gigasievert**	GSv

Unit names must not begin with a capital letter.

Prefixes must only be used when combined with a unit.

Symbols must remain unaltered in the plural. DO NOT ADD 's', "ms" refers to millisecond **not metres**.

gigasteradian	Gsr	**hectohertz**	hHz
gigatesla	GT	**hectojoule**	hJ
gigavolt	GV	**hectokelvin**	hK
gigawatt	GW	**hectolumen**	hlm
gigaweber	GWb	**hectolux**	hlx
gram	g	**hectometre**	hm
gray	Gy	**hectomole**	hmol
		hectonewton	hN
hecto +	*'h' ; 'hecto' is a*	**hectoohm**	hΩ
	prefix	**hectopascal**	hPa
hectoampere	hA	**hectoradian**	hrad
hectobecquerel	hBq	**hectosecond**	hs
hectocandela	hcd	**hectosiemens**	hS
hectocoulomb	hC	**hectosievert**	hSv
hectofarad	hF	**hectosteradian**	hsr
hectogram	hg	**hectotesla**	hT
hectogray	hGy	**hectovolt**	hV
hectohenry	hH	**hectowatt**	hW

Unit names must not begin with a capital letter.

Prefixes must only be used when combined with a unit.

---

*Symbols must remain unaltered in the plural. DO NOT ADD 's', "ms" refers to millisecond **not metres.***

---

hectoweber	hWb	**kilogray**	kGy
henry	H	**kilohenry**	kH
hertz	Hz	**kilohertz**	kHz
		kilojoule	kJ
joule	J	**kilokelvin**	kK
		kilolumen	klm
kelvin	K ; NOTE: it is	**kilolux**	klx
	incorrect to write	**kilometre**	km
	"°**K**" compare	**kilomole**	kmol
	"**degree Celsius**"	**kilonewton**	kN
	"°C"	**kiloohm**	kΩ
kilo +	*'k' ; 'kilo' is a prefix*	**kilopascal**	kPa
kiloampere	kA	**kiloradian**	krad
kilobecquerel	kBq	**kilosecond**	ks
kilocandela	kcd	**kilosiemens**	kS
kilocoulomb	kC	**kilosievert**	kSv
kilofarad	kF	**kilosteradian**	ksr
kilogram	kg	**kilotesla**	kT

> *Unit names must not begin with a capital letter.*

> *Prefixes must only be used when combined with a unit.*

> *Symbols must remain unaltered in the plural. DO NOT ADD 's', "ms" refers to millisecond **not metres.***

kilovolt	kV		**megajoule**	MJ
kilowatt	kW		**megakelvin**	MK
kiloweber	kWb		**megalumen**	Mlm
			megalux	Mlx
lumen	lm		**megametre**	Mm
lux	lx		**megamole**	Mmol
			meganewton	MN
mega +	*'M' ; mega is a*		**megaohm**	MΩ
	prefix		**megapascal**	MPa
megaampere	MA		**megaradian**	Mrad
megabecquerel	MBq		**megasecond**	Ms
megacandela	Mcd		**megasiemens**	MS
megacoulomb	MC		**megasievert**	MSv
megafarad	MF		**megasteradian**	Msr
megagram	Mg		**megatesla**	MT
megagray	MGy		**megavolt**	MV
megahenry	MH		**megawatt**	MW
megahertz	MHz		**megaweber**	MWb

> Unit names must not begin with a capital letter.

> Prefixes must only be used when combined with a unit.

> Symbols must remain unaltered in the plural. DO NOT ADD 's', "ms" refers to millisecond **not metres**.

metre	m	**micronewton**	μN
micro +	*'μ' ; 'micro' is a*	**microohm**	μΩ
	prefix	**micropascal**	μPa
microampere	μA	**microradian**	μrad
microbecquerel	μBq	**microsecond**	μs
microcandela	μcd	**microsiemens**	μS
microcoulomb	μC	**microsievert**	μSv
microfarad	μF	**microsteradian**	μsr
microgram	μg	**microtesla**	μT
microgray	μGy	**microvolt**	μV
microhenry	μH	**microwatt**	μW
microhertz	μHz	**microweber**	μWb
microjoule	μJ	*milli +*	*'m' ; 'milli' is a*
microkelvin	μK		*prefix*
microlumen	μlm	**milliampere**	mA
microlux	μlx	**millibecquerel**	mBq
micrometre	μm	**millicandela**	mcd
micromole	μmol	**millicoulomb**	mC

Unit names must not begin with a capital letter.

Prefixes must only be used when combined with a unit.

Symbols must remain unaltered in the plural. DO NOT ADD 's', "ms" refers to millisecond **not metres**.

millifarad	mF	**millisteradian**	msr
milligram	mg	**millitesla**	mT
milligray	mGy	**millivolt**	mV
millihenry	mH	**milliwatt**	mW
millihertz	mHz	**milliweber**	mWb
millijoule	mJ	**mole**	mol
millikelvin	mK		
millilumen	mlm	*nano +*	*'n' ; 'nano' is a*
millilux	mlx		*prefix*
millimetre	mm	**nanoampere**	nA
millimole	mmol	**nanobecquerel**	nBq
millinewton	mN	**nanocandela**	ncd
milliohm	mΩ	**nanocoulomb**	nC
millipascal	mPa	**nanofarad**	nF
milliradian	mrad	**nanogram**	ng
millisecond	ms	**nanogray**	nGy
millisiemens	mS	**nanohenry**	nH
millisievert	mSv	**nanohertz**	nHz

Unit names must not begin with a capital letter.	

Prefixes must only be used when combined with a unit.	

*Symbols must remain unaltered in the plural. DO NOT ADD 's', "ms" refers to millisecond **not metres**.*	

nanojoule	nJ	**newton**	N
nanokelvin	nK		
nanolumen	nlm	**ohm**	Ω
nanolux	nlx		
nanometre	nm	**pascal**	Pa
nanomole	nmol	*peta +*	*'P' ; 'peta' is a*
nanonewton	nN		*prefix*
nanoohm	nΩ	**petaampere**	PA
nanopascal	nPa	**petabecquerel**	PBq
nanoradian	nrad	**petacandela**	Pcd
nanosecond	ns	**petacoulomb**	PC
nanosiemens	nS	**petafarad**	PF
nanosievert	nSv	**petagram**	Pg
nanosteradian	nsr	**petagray**	PGy
nanotesla	nT	**petahenry**	PH
nanovolt	nV	**petahertz**	PHz
nanowatt	nW	**petajoule**	PJ
nanoweber	nWb	**petakelvin**	PK

Unit names must not begin with a capital letter.	

Prefixes must only be used when combined with a unit.

*Symbols must remain unaltered in the plural. DO NOT ADD 's', "ms" refers to millisecond **not metres**.*

petalumen	Plm		**picoampere**	pA
petalux	Plx		**picobecquerel**	pBq
petametre	Pm		**picocandela**	pcd
petamole	Pmol		**picocoulomb**	pC
petanewton	PN		**picofarad**	pF
petaohm	PΩ		**picogram**	pg
petapascal	PPa		**picogray**	pGy
petaradian	Prad		**picohenry**	pH
petasecond	Ps		**picohertz**	pHz
petasiemens	PS		**picojoule**	pJ
petasievert	PSv		**picokelvin**	pK
petasteradian	Psr		**picolumen**	plm
petatesla	PT		**picolux**	plx
petavolt	PV		**picometre**	pm
petawatt	PW		**picomole**	pmol
petaweber	PWb		**piconewton**	pN
pico +	*'p' ; 'pico' is a*		**picoohm**	pΩ
	prefix		**picopascal**	pPa

Unit names must not begin with a capital letter.	

Prefixes must only be used when combined with a unit.	

*Symbols must remain unaltered in the plural. DO NOT ADD 's', "ms" refers to millisecond **not metres**.*	

picoradian	prad	*tera +*	*'T' ; 'tera' is a*
picosecond	ps		*prefix*
picosiemens	pS	**teraampere**	TA
picosievert	pSv	**terabecquerel**	TBq
picosteradian	psr	**teracandela**	Tcd
picotesla	pT	**teracoulomb**	TC
picovolt	pV	**terafarad**	TF
picowatt	pW	**teragram**	Tg
picoweber	pWb	**teragray**	TGy
		terahenry	TH
radian	rad	**terahertz**	THz
		terajoule	TJ
second	s	**terakelvin**	TK
siemens	S	**teralumen**	Tlm
sievert	Sv	**teralux**	Tlx
steradian	sr	**terametre**	Tm
		teramole	Tmol
		teranewton	TN

Unit names must not begin with a capital letter.

Prefixes must only be used when combined with a unit.

Symbols must remain unaltered in the plural. DO NOT ADD 's', "ms" refers to millisecond **not metres.**

teraohm	TΩ	*yocto +*	*'y' ; 'yocto' is a*
terapascal	TPa		*prefix*
teraradian	Trad	**yoctoampere**	yA
terasecond	Ts	**yoctobecquerel**	yBq
terasiemens	TS	**yoctocandela**	ycd
terasievert	TSv	**yoctocoulomb**	yC
terasteradian	Tsr	**yoctofarad**	yF
teratesla	TT	**yoctogram**	yg
teravolt	TV	**yoctogray**	yGy
terawatt	TW	**yoctohenry**	yH
teraweber	TWb	**yoctohertz**	yHz
tesla	T	**yoctojoule**	yJ
		yoctokelvin	yK
volt	V	**yoctolumen**	ylm
		yoctolux	ylx
watt	W	**yoctometre**	ym
weber	Wb	**yoctomole**	ymol
		yoctonewton	yN

> *Unit names must not begin with a capital letter.*

> *Prefixes must only be used when combined with a unit.*

> *Symbols must remain unaltered in the plural. DO NOT ADD 's', "ms" refers to millisecond **not metres**.*

yoctoohm	yΩ		**yottagram**	Yg
yoctopascal	yPa		**yottagray**	YGy
yoctoradian	yrad		**yottahenry**	YH
yoctosecond	ys		**yottahertz**	YHz
yoctosiemens	yS		**yottajoule**	YJ
yoctosievert	ySv		**yottakelvin**	YK
yoctosteradian	ysr		**yottalumen**	Ylm
yoctotesla	yT		**yottalux**	Ylx
yoctovolt	yV		**yottametre**	Ym
yoctowatt	yW		**yottamole**	Ymol
yoctoweber	yWb		**yottanewton**	YN
yotta +	'Y' ; 'yotta' is a		**yottaohm**	YΩ
	prefix		**yottapascal**	YPa
yottaampere	YA		**yottaradian**	Yrad
yottabecquerel	YBq		**yottasecond**	Ys
yottacandela	Ycd		**yottasiemens**	YS
yottacoulomb	YC		**yottasievert**	YSv
yottafarad	YF		**yottasteradian**	Ysr

> *Unit names must not begin with a capital letter.*

> *Prefixes must only be used when combined with a unit.*

> *Symbols must remain unaltered in the plural. DO NOT ADD 's', "ms" refers to millisecond* **not metres.**

yottatesla	YT	**zeptolumen**	zlm
yottavolt	YV	**zeptolux**	zlx
yottawatt	YW	**zeptometre**	zm
yottaweber	YWb	**zeptomole**	zmol
		zeptonewton	zN
zepto +	*'z' ; zepto is a*	**zeptoohm**	zΩ
	prefix	**zeptopascal**	zPa
zeptoampere	zA	**zeptoradian**	zrad
zeptobecquerel	zBq	**zeptosecond**	zs
zeptocandela	zcd	**zeptosiemens**	zS
zeptocoulomb	zC	**zeptosievert**	zSv
zeptofarad	zF	**zeptosteradian**	zsr
zeptogram	zg	**zeptotesla**	zT
zeptogray	zGy	**zeptovolt**	zV
zeptohenry	zH	**zeptowatt**	zW
zeptohertz	zHz	**zeptoweber**	zWb
zeptojoule	zJ	*zetta +*	*'Z' ; zetta is a*
zeptokelvin	zK		*prefix*

Unit names must not begin with a capital letter.

Prefixes must only be used when combined with a unit.

Symbols must remain unaltered in the plural. DO NOT ADD 's', "ms" refers to millisecond **not metres**.

zettaampere	ZA	**zettaradian**	Zrad
zettabecquerel	ZBq	**zettasecond**	Zs
zettacandela	Zcd	**zettasiemens**	ZS
zettacoulomb	ZC	**zettasievert**	ZSv
zettafarad	ZF	**zettasteradian**	Zsr
zettagram	Zg	**zettatesla**	ZT
zettagray	ZGy	**zettavolt**	ZV
zettahenry	ZH	**zettawatt**	ZW
zettahertz	ZHz	**zettaweber**	ZWb
zettajoule	ZJ		
zettakelvin	ZK		
zettalumen	Zlm		
zettalux	Zlx		
zettametre	Zm		
zettamole	Zmol		
zettanewton	ZN		
zettaohm	ZΩ		
zettapascal	ZPa		

SI UNITS NAMED AFTER SCIENTISTS

SYMBOL	UNIT	QUANTITY	SCIENTIST		
A	ampere	electric current, magnetic potential difference	André Marie Ampère	1775–1836	French
Bq	becquerel	Radioactivity (activity of a radionuclide)	Antoine Henri Becquerel	1852–1908	French
C	coulomb	electric charge, quantity of electricity	Charles Augustin de Coulomb	1736–1806	French
°C	degree Celsius	temperature [SPECIAL NAME FOR THE UNIT KELVIN]	Anders Celsius	1701–1744	Swedish
F	farad	capacitance	Michael Faraday	1791–1867	British
Gy	gray	absorbed dose of radiation, kerma	Louis Harold Gray	1905–1965	British
H	henry	inductance	Joseph Henry	1797–1878	American

SI UNITS NAMED AFTER SCIENTISTS (continued)

SYMBOL	UNIT	QUANTITY	SCIENTIST		
Hz	hertz	frequency	Heinrich Rudolf Hertz	1857–1894	German
J	joule	energy, work, heat	James Prescott Joule	1818–1889	British
K	kelvin	thermodynamic temperature	Lord Kelvin (William Thomson)	1824–1907	British
N	newton	force	Sir Isaac Newton	1642–1727	British
Ω	ohm	resistance, impedance, reactance	Georg Simon Ohm	1787–1854	German
Pa	pascal	pressure, stress	Blaise Pascal	1623–1662	French
S	siemens	conductance, admittance, susceptance	Ernst Werner von Siemens	1816–1892	German
Sv	sievert	dose equivalent of radiation	Rolf Maximilian Sievert	1896–1960	Swedish

SI UNITS NAMED AFTER SCIENTISTS (continued)

SYMBOL	UNIT	QUANTITY	SCIENTIST		
T	tesla	magnetic flux density, magnetic induction, magnetic polarization	Nikola Tesla	1857–1943	American
V	volt	electrical potential, tension, electromotive force	Alessandro Volta	1745–1827	Italian
W	watt	power, radiant energy flux, heat flow rate	James Watt	1736–1819	British
Wb	weber	magnetic flux	Wilhelm Eduard Weber	1804–1891	German

PART TWO

Setting a Standard

Metric-Matters, in line with an international suggestion, recommends that only certain multiples and submultiples of SI units are used. The following example illustrates if the number of prefixes used is limited, the values presented can become more meaningful.

EXAMPLE
Original data using
a variety of prefixes

BETTER ALTERNATIVES FOR THE
PRESENTATION OF THE DATA

ELECTRIC CURRENT

		ELECTRIC CURRENT			
700,00	dA	70	A	7×10^4	mA
7,00	hA	700	A	7×10^5	mA
8,00	kA	8 000	A	8×10^6	mA
700,00	cA	7	A	7×10^3	mA
0,80	daA	8	A	8×10^3	mA

Please Note: in the above values a comma is the international standard way to show the decimal marker/sign.

In this part of the dictionary the suggested selection of units (with prefixes) caters for advanced students and also for browsers.

Metric-Matters is aware that some enthusiasts may regard the international recommendations as being restrictive. There is still freedom to explore incredibly small areas (UNIT: **zm²**) and disappear into vast volumes and discover a very unusual solution (UNIT: **ymol/Ym³**).

Listing by Symbol

SYMBOL	UNIT NAME	QUANTITY
A	ampere	electric current, magnetic potential difference
A/cm	ampere per centimetre	linear electric current density, lineic electric current, magnetic field strength
A/cm²	ampere per square centimetre	areic electric current, electric current density
A/m	ampere per metre	linear electric current density, lineic electric current, magnetic field strength, magnetization
A•m²	ampere square metre	electromagnetic moment, magnetic moment
A/m²	ampere per square metre	areic electric current, electric current density
A/mm	ampere per millimetre	linear electric current density, lineic electric current, magnetic field strength, magnetization
A/mm²	ampere per square millimetre	areic electric current, electric current density
aJ	attojoule	gap energy
Bq	becquerel	activity
Bq/kg	becquerel per kilogram	massic activity, specific activity

SYMBOL	UNIT NAME	QUANTITY
C	coulomb	electric charge, electric flux, quantity of electricity
C/cm²	coulomb per square centimetre	areic charge, electric flux density, electric polarization, surface density of charge
C/cm³	coulomb per cubic centimetre	charge density, volume density of charge, volumic charge
C/kg	coulomb per kilogram	exposure
C•m	coulomb metre	electric dipole moment
C/m²	coulomb per square metre	areic charge, electric flux density, electric polarization, surface density of charge
C/m³	coulomb per cubic metre	charge density, volumic charge, volume density of charge
C/mm²	coulomb per square millimetre	areic charge, surface density of charge
C/mm³	coulomb per cubic millimetre	charge density, volume density of charge, volumic charge
°C	degree Celsius	Celsius temperature
cd	candela	luminous intensity
cd/m²	candela per square metre	luminance
cm	centimetre	length
cm²	square centimetre	area
cm³	cubic centimetre	volume

SYMBOL	UNIT NAME	QUANTITY
cm³/mol	cubic centimetre per mole	molar volume
dm²	square decimetre	area
dm³	cubic decimetre	volume
dm³/mol	cubic decimetre per mole	molar volume
EJ	exajoule	energy, heat, work
F	farad	capacitance
F/m	farad per metre	permittivity
fJ	femtojoule	gap energy
fm	femtometre	length
Gy	gray	absorbed dose
GC/m³	gigacoulomb per cubic metre	charge density, volume density of charge, volumic density
GHz	gigahertz	frequency
GJ	gigajoule	active energy, energy, heat, work
GΩ	gigaohm	resistance
GΩ•m	gigaohm metre	resistivity
GPa	gigapascal	normal stress, pressure
GW	gigawatt	active power, power
g	gram	mass
g/cm³	gram per cubic centimetre	density, mass density, volumic mass
g/mol	gram per mole	molar mass
H	henry	mutual inductance, self-inductance, permeance

SYMBOL	UNIT NAME	QUANTITY
H⁻¹	'reciprocal henry', 'per henry'	reluctance
H/m	henry per metre	permeability
Hz	hertz	frequency
hPa	hectopascal	pressure
J	joule	active energy, energy, gap energy, heat, radiant energy, reaction energy, work
J/K	joule per kelvin	entropy, heat capacity
J/kg	joule per kilogram	massic thermodynamic energy
J/(kg•K)	joule per kilogram kelvin	massic entropy, massic heat capacity
J⁻¹/m³	'reciprocal joule per cubic metre' 'per joule per cubic metre'	density of states
J/mol	joule per mole	molar thermodynamic energy
J/(mol•K)	joule per mole kelvin	molar entropy, molar heat capacity
K	kelvin	Curie temperature, thermodynamic temperature
K⁻¹	'reciprocal kelvin', 'per kelvin'	linear expansion coefficient
kA	kiloampere	electric current, magnetic potential difference
kA/m	kiloampere per metre	linear electric current density, lineic electric current, magnetic field strength, magnetization

SYMBOL	UNIT NAME	QUANTITY
kA/m^2	kiloampere per square metre	areic electric current, electric current density
kBq	kilobecquerel	activity
kBq/kg	kilobecquerel per kilogram	massic activity, specific activity
kC	kilocoulomb	electric charge, electric flux, quantity of electricity
kC/m^2	kilocoulomb per square metre	areic charge, electric flux density, electric polarization, surface density of charge
kC/m^3	kilocoulomb per cubic metre	charge density, volume density of charge, volumic charge
kg	kilogram	mass, mass defect
kg/dm^3	kilogram per cubic decimetre	density, mass density, volumic mass
kg/m	kilogram per metre	linear density, lineic mass
$kg•m^2$	kilogram square metre	moment of inertia
kg/m^3	kilogram per cubic metre	density, mass density, volumic mass
kg/mol	kilogram per mole	molar mass
kg•m/s	kilogram metre per second	momentum
$kg•m^2/s$	kilogram square metre per second	angular momentum, moment of momentum
kHz	kilohertz	frequency
kJ	kilojoule	active energy, energy, heat, work

SYMBOL	UNIT NAME	QUANTITY
kJ/K	kilojoule per kelvin	entropy, heat capacity
kJ/kg	kilojoule per kilogram	massic thermodynamic energy
kJ/ (kg•K)	kilojoule per kilogram kelvin	massic entropy, massic heat capacity
kJ/mol	kilojoule per mole	thermodynamic energy
km	kilometre	length
km²	square kilometre	area
kmol	kilomole	amount of substance
kmol/m³	kilomole per cubic metre	amount-of-substance concentration, concentration
kN	kilonewton	force
kN•m	kilonewton metre	moment of force
kΩ	kiloohm	impedance, reactance, resistance
kΩ•m	kiloohm metre	resistivity
kPa	kilopascal	normal stress, pressure
kS	kilosiemens	admittance, conductance, susceptance
kS/m	kilosiemens per metre	conductivity
ks	kilosecond	time
kV	kilovolt	electric potential, electromotive force, potential difference, tension
kV/m	kilovolt per metre	electric field strength
kW	kilowatt	active power, heat flow rate, power, sound power

SYMBOL	UNIT NAME	QUANTITY
kWb/m	kiloweber per metre	magnetic vector potential
lm	lumen	luminous flux
lm/m²	lumen per square metre	luminous exitance
lm•s	lumen second	quantity of light
lm/W	lumen per watt	luminous efficacy
lx	lux	illuminance
lx•s	lux second	light exposure
m	metre	length, wavelength
m²	square metre	area, equivalent absorption area of a surface or object
m³	cubic metre	volume
m³/C	cubic metre per coulomb	Hall coefficient
m²•K/W	square metre kelvin per watt	thermal insulance
m³/mol	cubic metre per mole	molar volume
m/s	metre per second	velocity, velocity of sound, sound particle velocity
m/s²	'metre per second squared'	acceleration
m²/s	square metre per second	diffusion coefficient, kinematic viscosity, thermal diffusion coefficient
m³/s	cubic metre per second	volume flow rate
mol	mole	amount of substance

SYMBOL	UNIT NAME	QUANTITY
mol/dm³	mole per cubic decimetre	amount-of-substance concentration, concentration
mol/kg	mole per kilogram	molality of solute
mol/m³	mole per cubic metre	amount-of-substance concentration, concentration
MA/m²	megaampere per square metre	areic electric current, electric current density
MBq	megabecquerel	activity
MBq/kg	megabecquerel per kilogram	massic activity, specific activity
MC	megacoulomb	electric flux
MC/m²	megacoulomb per square metre	areic charge, surface density of charge
MC/m³	megacoulomb per cubic metre	charge density, volume density of charge, volumic charge
Mg	megagram	mass
Mg/m³	megagram per cubic metre	density, mass density, volumic mass
MHz	megahertz	frequency
MJ	megajoule	active energy, energy, heat, work
MJ/kg	megajoule per kilogram	massic thermodynamic energy
MN	meganewton	force
MN•m	meganewton metre	moment of force
MΩ	megaohm	impedance, reactance, resistance

SYMBOL	UNIT NAME	QUANTITY
MΩ•m	megaohm metre	resistivity
MPa	megapascal	normal stress, pressure
MS/m	megasiemens per metre	conductivity
MV	megavolt	electric potential, electromotive force, potential difference, tension
MV/m	megavolt per metre	electric field strength
MW	megawatt	active power, power
mA	milliampere	electric current, magnetic potential difference
mC	millicoulomb	electric flux
mC/kg	millicoulomb per kilogram	exposure
mC/m²	millicoulomb per square metre	areic charge, electric flux density, electric polarization, surface density of charge
mC/m³	millicoulomb per cubic metre	charge density, volume density of charge, volumic charge
mF	millifarad	capacitance
mGy	milligray	absorbed dose
mg	milligram	mass
mg/m	milligram per metre	linear density, lineic mass
mH	millihenry	mutual inductance, self-inductance
mJ	millijoule	energy, heat, work

SYMBOL	UNIT NAME	QUANTITY
mm	millimetre	length, wavelength
mm²	square millimetre	area
mm³	cubic millimetre	volume
mm/s	millimetre per second	sound particle velocity
mm²/s	square millimetre per second	kinematic viscosity
mmol	millimole	amount of substance
mmol/kg	millimole per kilogram	molality of solute
mN	millinewton	force
mN/m	millinewton per metre	surface tension
mN•m	millinewton metre	moment of force
mΩ	milliohm	impedance, reactance, resistance
mΩ•m	milliohm metre	resistivity
mPa	millipascal	pressure, sound pressure, static pressure
mPa•s	millipascal second	dynamic viscosity
mrad	milliradian	plane angle
mS	millisiemens	admittance, conductance, susceptance
ms	millisecond	half-life, period, periodic time, time
mSv	millisievert	dose equivalent
mT	millitesla	magnetic flux density, magnetic induction, magnetic polarization

SYMBOL	UNIT NAME	QUANTITY
mV	millivolt	electric potential, electromotive force, potential difference, tension, thermoelectromotive force
mV/K	millivolt per kelvin	Thomson coefficient
mV/m	millivolt per metre	electric field strength
mW	milliwatt	active power, power, sound power
mW/m^2	milliwatt per square metre	sound intensity
mWb	milliweber	magnetic flux
μA	microampere	electric current
μC	microcoulomb	electric charge, quantity of electricity
μC/m^2	microcoulomb per square metre	areic charge, electric flux density, electric polarization, surface density of charge
μC/m^3	microcoulomb per cubic metre	charge density, volume density of charge, volumic charge
μF	microfarad	capacitance
μF/m	microfarad per metre	permittivity
μg	microgram	mass
μH	microhenry	mutual inductance, self-inductance
μH/m	microhenry per metre	permeability
μm	micrometre	length, wavelength
μmol	micromole	amount of substance

SYMBOL	UNIT NAME	QUANTITY
*μ*N	micronewton	force
*μ*N•m	micronewton metre	moment of force
*μ*Ω	microohm	resistance
*μ*Ω•m	microohm metre	resistivity
*μ*Pa	micropascal	pressure, sound pressure, static pressure
*μ*rad	microradian	plane angle
*μ*S	microsiemens	admittance, conductance, susceptance
*μ*s	microsecond	period, periodic time, time
*μ*T	microtesla	magnetic flux density, magnetic induction
*μ*V	microvolt	electric potential, electromotive force, potential difference, tension
*μ*V/m	microvolt per metre	electric field strength
*μ*W	microwatt	active power, power, sound power
*μ*W/m^2	microwatt per square metre	sound intensity
N	newton	force
N/m	newton per metre	surface tension
N•m	newton metre	moment of force
N•m^2/A	newton square metre per ampere	magnetic dipole moment
N•s/m	newton second per metre	mechanical impedance

SYMBOL	UNIT NAME	QUANTITY
nA	nanoampere	electric current
nC	nanocoulomb	electric charge, quantity of electricity
nF	nanofarad	capacitance
nF/m	nanofarad per metre	permittivity
nH	nanohenry	mutual inductance, self-inductance
nH/m	nanohenry per metre	permeability
nm	nanometre	length, wavelength
nΩ•m	nanoohm metre	resistivity
ns	nanosecond	time
nT	nanotesla	magnetic flux density, magnetic induction
nW	nanowatt	active power
Ω	ohm	impedance, reactance, resistance
Ω•cm	ohm centimetre	resistivity
Ω•m	ohm metre	resistivity
Pa	pascal	normal stress, pressure, sound pressure, static pressure
Pa•s	pascal second	viscosity (dynamic viscosity)
Pa•s/m	pascal second per metre	surface density of mechanical impedance
Pa•s/m^3	pascal second per cubic metre	acoustic impedance
PJ	petajoule	energy, heat, work

SYMBOL	UNIT NAME	QUANTITY
pA	petaampere	electric current
pC	petacoulomb	electric charge, quantity of electricity
pF	petafarad	capacitance
pF/m	petafarad per metre	permittivity
pH	petahenry	mutual inductance, self-inductance
pm	petametre	length, wavelength
pW	petawatt	sound power
pW/m^2	petawatt per square metre	sound intensity
rad	radian	plane angle
rad/s	radian per second	angular frequency, angular velocity
S	siemens	admittance, conductance, susceptance
S/m	siemens per metre	conductivity
s	second	half-life, period, periodic time, reverberation time, time
s^{-1}	'reciprocal second', 'per second'	rotational frequency
sr	steradian	solid angle
Sv	sievert	dose equivalent
T	tesla	magnetic flux density, magnetic induction, magnetic polarization
THz	terahertz	frequency

SYMBOL	UNIT NAME	QUANTITY
TJ	terajoule	active energy, erergy, heat, work
TW	terawatt	active power
V	volt	electric potential, electromotive force, potential difference, tension, thermoelectromotive force
V/cm	volt per centimetre	electric field strength
V/K	volt per kelvin	Thomson coefficient
V/m	volt per metre	electric field strength
V/mm	volt per millimetre	electric field strength
W	watt	active power, heat flow rate, power, radiant energy flux, radiant power, sound power
W/m²	watt per square metre	irradiance, radiant exitance, sound intensity
W/(m•K)	watt per metre kelvin	thermal conductivity
W/(m²•K)	watt per square metre kelvin	coefficient of heat transfer
W/sr	watt per steradian	radiant intensity
W/(sr•m²)	watt per steradian square metre	radiance
Wb	weber	magnetic flux
Wb•m	weber metre	magnetic dipole moment
Wb/m	weber per metre	magnetic vector potential

SYMBOL	UNIT NAME	QUANTITY
Wb/mm	weber per millimetre	magnetic vector potential
1	} CHARACTERISTIC	Mach number
1	} } NUMBERS	Reynolds number

Listing by Quantity

A RECOMMENDED SELECTION OF UNITS (WITH PREFIXES), HELPFUL WHEN PRESENTING VALUES, [For more detailed information refer to sources given in the bibliography.]

absorbed dose	active power	admittance
Gy	TW	kS
mGy	GW	S
	MW	mS
acceleration	kW	μS
m/s^2	W	
	mW	**amount of substance**
acoustic impedance	μW	kmol
Pa•s/m^3	nW	mol
		mmol
active energy	**activity**	μmol
TJ	MBq	
GJ	kBq	**amount-of-substance**
MJ	Bq	**concentration**
kJ		mol/dm^3 or kmol/m^3
J		mol/m^3

angle:	areic charge	charge density
plane angle	MC/m^2 or C/mm^2	C/mm^3 or GC/m^3
rad	C/cm^2	MC/m^3 or C/cm^3
mrad	kC/m^2	kC/m^3
μrad	mC/m^2	C/m^3
	$\mu C/m^2$	mC/m^3
solid angle		$\mu C/m^3$
sr	**areic electric current**	
	MA/m^2 or A/mm^2	**coefficient of heat**
angular frequency	A/cm^2	**transfer**
rad/s	kA/m^2	$W/(m^2 \bullet K)$
	A/m^2	
angular momentum		**concentration**
$kg \bullet m^2/s$	**capacitance**	mol/dm^3 or $kmol/m^3$
	F	mol/m^3
angular velocity	mF	
rad/s	μF	**conductance**
	nF	kS
area	pF	S
km^2		mS
m^2	**Celsius temperature**	μS
dm^2	$^\circ$C	
cm^2		
mm^2		

conductivity	electric charge	electric field strength
MS/m	kC	MV/m
kS/m	C	kV/m or V/mm
S/m	μC	V/cm
	nC	V/m
Curie temperature	pC	mV/m
K		μV/m
	electric current	
density	kA	**electric flux**
Mg/m^3 or kg/dm^3	A	MC
or g/cm^3	mA	kC
kg/m^3	μA	C
	nA	mC
density of states	pA	
J^{-1}/m^3		**electric flux density**
	electric current density	C/cm^2
diffusion coefficient	MA/m^2 or A/mm^2	kC/m^2
m^2/s	A/cm^2	C/m^2
	kA/m^2	mC/m^2
dose equivalent	A/m^2	μC/m^2
Sv		
mSv	**electric dipole moment**	
	C•m	

electric polarization	energy	force
C/cm^2	EJ	MN
kC/m^2	PJ	kN
C/m^2	TJ	N
mC/m^2	GJ	mN
μC/m^2	MJ	μN
	kJ	
electric potential	J	**frequency**
MV	mJ	THz
kV		GHz
V	**entropy**	MHz
mV	kJ/K	kHz
μV	J/K	Hz
electromagnetic moment	**equivalent absorption area of a surface or object**	**gap energy**
		J
A•m^2		fJ
	m^2	aJ
electromotive force		
MV	**exposure**	**half-life**
kV	C/kg	s
V	mC/kg	ms
mV		
μV		

Hall coeficient	impedance	length
m³/C	MΩ	km
	kΩ	m
heat	Ω	cm
EJ	mΩ	mm
PJ		µm
TJ	**inductance**	nm
GJ	H	pm
MJ	mH	fm
kJ	µH	
J	nH	**light exposure**
mJ	pH	lx•s
heat flow rate	**irradiance**	**linear density**
kW	W/m²	kg/m
W		mg/m
heat capacity		**linear electric current**
kJ/K		**density**
J/K		kA/m or A/mm
		A/cm
illuminance		A/m
lx		

linear expansion coefficient	luminous intensity	magnetic induction
K^{-1}	cd	T
		mT
	Mach number	μT
lineic electric current	1	nT
kA/m or A/mm		
A/cm	**magnetic dipole**	**magnetic moment**
A/m	**moment**	A•m^2
	N•m^2/A or Wb•m	
lineic mass		**magnetic polarization**
kg/m	**magnetic field strength**	T
mg/m	kA/m or A/mm	mT
	A/cm	
luminance	A/m	**magnetic potential**
cd/m^2		**difference**
	magnetic flux	kA
luminous efficacy	Wb	A
lm/W	mWb	mA
luminous exitance	**magnetic flux density**	**magnetic vector**
lm/m^2	T	**potential**
	mT	kWb/m or Wb/mm
luminous flux	μT	Wb/m
lm	nT	

magnetization	massic entropy	modulus of impedance
kA/m or A/mm	kJ/(kg•K)	MΩ
A/m	J/(kg•K)	kΩ
		Ω
mass	**massic heat capacity**	mΩ
Mg	kJ/(kg•K)	
kg	J/(kg•K)	**molality of solute**
g		mol/kg
mg	**massic thermodynamic**	mmol/kg
μg	**energy**	
	MJ/kg	**molar entropy**
mass defect	kJ/kg	J/(mol•K)
kg	J/kg	
		molar heat capacity
mass density	**mechanical impedance**	J/(mol•K)
Mg/m³ or kg/dm³	N•s/m	
or g/cm³		**molar mass**
kg/m³	**modulus of admittance**	kg/mol
	kS	g/mol
massic activity	S	
MBq/kg	mS	**molar thermodynamic**
kBq/kg	μS	**energy**
Bq/kg		kJ/mol
		J/mol

molar volume	normal stress	permittivity
m^3/mol	GPa	F/m
dm^3/mol	MPa	μF/m
cm^3/mol	kPa	nF/m
	Pa	pF/m
moment of force		
MN•m	**period**	**potential difference**
kN•m	s	MV
N•m	ms	kV
mN•m	μs	V
μN•m		mV
	periodic time	μV
moment of inertia	s	
kg•m^2	ms	**power**
	μs	GW
moment of momentum		MW
kg•m^2/s	**permeability**	kW
	H/m	W
momentum	μH/m	mW
kg•m/s	nH/m	μW
	permeance	
	H	

pressure	radiant energy flux	resistance
GPa	W	GΩ
MPa		MΩ
kPa	**radiant exitance**	kΩ
hPa	W/m²	Ω
Pa		mΩ
mPa	**radiant intensity**	μΩ
μPa	W/sr	
		resistivity
quantity of electricity	**radiant power**	GΩ•m
kC	W	MΩ•m
C		kΩ•m
μC	**reactance**	Ω•m
nC	MΩ	Ω•cm
pC	kΩ	mΩ•m
	Ω	μΩ•m
quantity of light	mΩ	nΩ•m
lm•s		
	reaction energy	**reverberation time**
radiance	J	s
W/(sr•m²)		
	reluctance	**Reynolds number**
radiant energy	H⁻¹	1
J		

rotational frequency	sound pressure	surface tension
s^{-1}	Pa	N/m
	mPa	mN/m
specific activity	μPa	
MBq/kg		**susceptance**
kBq/kg	**static pressure**	kS
Bq/kg	Pa	S
	MPa	mS
sound intensity	μPa	μS
W/m²		
mW/m²	**surface density of**	**tension**
μW/m²	**charge**	MV
pW/m²	MC/m²	kV
	or C/mm²	V
sound particle velocity	C/cm²	mV
m/s	kC/m²	μV
mm/s	C/m²	
	mC/m²	**thermal conductivity**
sound power	μC/m²	W(m•K)
kW		
W	**surface density of**	**thermal diffusion**
mW	**mechanical**	**coefficient**
	impedance	
μW	Pa•s/m	m²/s
pW		

thermal insulance	velocity	volume density of
$m^2 \cdot K/W$	m/s	**charge**
		C/mm^3 or GC/m^3
thermodynamic	**viscosity:**	MC/m^3 or C/cm^3
temperature	**dynamic viscosity**	kC/m^3
K	Pa•s	C/m^3
	mPa•s	mC/m^3
thermoelectromotive		$\mu C/m^3$
force	**kinematic viscosity**	
V	m^2/s	**volume flow rate**
mV	mm^2s	m^3/s
Thomson coefficient	**volume**	**volumic charge**
V/K	m^3	C/mm^3 or GC/m^3
mV/K	dm^3	MC/m^3 or C/cm^3
	cm^3	kC/m^3
time	mm^3	C/m^3
ks		mC/m^3
s		$\mu C/m^3$
ms		
μs		**volumic mass**
ns		Mg/m^3 or kg/dm^3
		or g/cm^3
		kg/m^3

wavelength

m

mm

μm

nm

pm

work

EJ

PJ

TJ

GJ

MJ

kJ

J

mJ

SI Prefixes and Factors

Prefix		Factor
Name	**Symbol**	
yotta	Y	10^{24}
zetta	Z	10^{21}
exa	E	10^{18}
peta	P	10^{15}
tera	T	10^{12}
giga	G	10^{9}
mega	M	10^{6}
kilo	k	10^{3}
hecto	h	10^{2}
deca	da	10
deci	d	10^{-1}
centi	c	10^{-2}
milli	m	10^{-3}
micro	μ	10^{-6}
nano	n	10^{-9}
pico	p	10^{-12}
femto	f	10^{-15}
atto	a	10^{-18}
zepto	z	10^{-21}
yocto	y	10^{-24}

Rules for Writing SI Units and Numerical Values

Metric-Matters encourages the use of recommendations made by the International Organisation for Standardization (ISO). The following examples give general guidance to show what is acceptable and what to avoid. For more detailed advice ISO publications should be consulted.

Writing Unit Names

1. Avoid using capital letters:
    ampere refers to the unit named after the scientist André Marie <u>Ampère.</u>

    It may be better to rewrite a sentence to avoid capitalization of a unit name.
    Example:
    not "Hertz, symbol 'Hz' is the unit of frequency."
    write instead "The unit for frequency is 'hertz' symbol 'Hz'."

2. Avoid use of the plural.
    In the presentation of data, examples:

Distance	=	65 kilometre	*not* kilometres
Area	=	5 square millimetre	*not* square millimetres
Volume	=	0.6 cubic metre	*not* cubic metres

    In sentences the use of plurals is acceptable, examples:
    'The distance between the two places is 65 kilometres.'
    'It covered an area of 5 square millimetres.'
    Note: **'siemens'** (symbol 'S') is singular and plural.

3.   Use only one prefix per unit.
      Example: 8 000 000   pascal
                    8 000   kilopascal
                  8 x 10^3 kilopascal
                         8   megapascal
                  not 8 kilokilopascal

Writing Symbols

1.   Take special care to write the correct-sized character.
      Examples:
      'PC'   means   'petacoulomb'   [10^{15} coulomb]
      'pC'   means   'picocoulomb'   [10^{-12} coulomb]
      'K'   means   'kelvin' : a temperature unit
      'k'   means   'kilo' : a prefix for 10^3

2.   Do not attempt to use plurals.
      Example:
      "3 ms" means three milliseconds
      "3 ms" does **not** mean three metres

3.   Take care with spaces, dots, hyphens and using a solidus (/).
      Examples:
      '10 N'   refers to 'ten newton'
      '10N'   may resemble a word (ion)
      'Wb•m'   refers to 'weber metre'
      'Wb/m'   refers to 'weber per metre'

The half-high dot means multiplication and is used in compound units.
'Wb/m', 'weber per metre' can also be written 'Wb•m^{-1}'

Where necessary parentheses (often called brackets) should be used to avoid ambiguity.

•   Full stops (periods) should **not** be written except in text to mark the end of a sentence.
•   Hyphens; only use a hyphen when writing names of units to avoid any ambiguity.

Writing Numerical Values

1. The decimal sign (or called decimal marker).
    Throughout the World this is written in several different ways.

    Example:
    One and a half (1 ½) expressed as

1,5	1.5	1•5
USE OF A COMMA	USE OF A DOT ON THE LINE	USE OF A HALF-HIGH DOT

    The decimal sign should be preceded by zero or another digit.
    Examples:
    a quarter (¼)   :   0,25
    six and a quarter (6 ¼):   6,25

2. A comma should **not** be used to show 'thousands' because misunderstandings could occur as the following example shows:
    2,345 means 'two point three four five' (2 345/1000)
    two thousand three hundred and forty five should be written:
    2 345

3. Spacing between groups of digits.
    One space should be left between each group of three digits.
    Example:
    2,346 x 10^6 written in full [showing four zeros after the decimal sign]
    2 346 000,000 0

4.   Choice of prefix.
     The most suitable prefix is chosen so that the numerical value before the symbol is between 0,1 and 1 000.
     Examples:

200 000	A		
2×10^5	A		
200	kA	}	preferred
0,2	MA	}	method
0,000 04	m		
4×10^{-5}	m		
4×10^{-2}	mm		
0,4	μm	}	preferred
400,0	nm	}	method
0,896 5	kg	}	preferred
896,5	g	}	method
$8,965 \times 10^{-1}$	kg		

Note

When considering values of the same quantity together it is often more helpful to use the **same** prefix even though some of the values may be less than 0,1 and greater than 1 000.

In some situations it may be more appropriate to express values using powers of ten instead of using prefixes.

Definitions of the Base Units
of the International System of Units

ampere: The ampere is that constant current which, if maintained in two straight parallel conductors of infinite length, of negligible circular cross-section, and placed 1 metre apart in vacuum, would produce between these conductors a force equal to 2 x 10^{-7} newton per metre of length.

candela: The candela is the luminous intensity, in a given direction, of a source that emits monochromatic radiation of frequency 540 x 10^{12} hertz and that has a radiant intensity in that direction of 1/683 watt per steradian.

kelvin: The kelvin, unit of thermodynamic temperature, is the fraction 1/273,16 of the thermodynamic temperature of the triple point of water.

The unit kelvin and its symbol K should be used to express an interval or a difference of temperature.

In addition to the thermodynamic temperature expressed in kelvins, use is also made of Celsius temperature. To express Celsius temperature, the unit "**degree Celsius**", which is equal to the unit "kelvin", is used; in this case, "**degree Celsius**" is a special name used in place of "**kelvin**". An interval or difference of Celsius temperature can, however, be expressed in kelvins as well as in degrees Celsius.

kilogram: The kilogram is the unit of mass; it is equal to the mass of the international prototype of the kilogram.

metre: The metre is the length of the path travelled by light in vacuum during a time interval of 1/299 792 458 of a second.

mole: The mole is the amount of substance of a system which contains as many elementary entities as there are atoms in 0,012 kilograms of carbon-12. When the mole is used, the elementary entities must be specified and may be atoms, molecules, ions, electrons, other particles, or specified groups of such particles.

second: The second is the duration of 9 192 631 770 periods of the radiation corresponding to the transition between the two hyperfine levels of the ground state of the caesium-133 atom.

BIBLIOGRAPHY

Suggested reference sources for more information include:

Le Système International d'Unités (SI)
(Approved English Translation)
United Kingdom editor: R J Bell
Pub. London: HMSO
ISBN 0 11 887538 8

International Standard ISO 31 (1992)/1000 (1992)
International Organization for Standardization
www.iso.org

Bureau International des Poids et Mesures
www.bipm.org

Dictionary of Scientific Units by H G Jerrard & D B McNeill
Pub: CHAPMAN & HALL, ISBN 0 412 46720 8

APPENDIX ONE

METRIC UNITS NOT STRICTLY SI UNITS

There are a few common metric units outside SI that are officially recognised.

UNIT	SYMBOL	QUANTITY	COMMENT
hectare*	ha*	area	1 ha = $10^4\,m^2$ *For temporary use only. Avoid using this unit.
litre	l, L	volume	The litre is a special name for the cubic decimetre (dm^3). No decision has been made yet which of the two symbols will be phased out.
tonne	t	mass	1t = 10^3 kg

APPENDIX TWO

ADDRESS FOR CORRESPONDENCE

SI Metric-Matters™

$^c/_o$ Diadem Books
Rose Cottage
South Laggan
Spean Bridge
PH34 4EA
U K

More more information see
www.diadembooks.com/metric.htm

978-0-595-37115-0
0-595-37115-9

Printed in the United Kingdom
by Lightning Source UK Ltd.
107829UKS00001B/286-336